RAILWAY HISTORY IN PICTURES

The British Railway Station

G. BIDDLE and JEOFFRY SPENCE

Drawings by PETER FELLS

DAVID & CHARLES

NEWTON ABBOT LONDON NORTH POMFRET (VT) VANCOUVER

ISBN 0 7153 7467 2

Library of Congress Catalog Card Number 77–89382

© Gordon Biddle and Jeoffry Spence 1977

Photoset in 10 on 11pt Times
and printed in Great Britain
by Redwood Burn Ltd
for David & Charles (Publishers) Limited
Brunel House Newton Abbot Devon

Published in the United States of America
by David & Charles Inc
North Pomfret Vermont 05053 USA

Published in Canada
by Douglas David & Charles Limited
1875 Welch Street North Vancouver BC

CONTENTS

Photographs not otherwise credited have been taken by the authors, or are from their collections.

FOREWORD

This book not only shows much of the development of the British railway station in its immense and unique variety, but also tries to re-create some of the atmosphere and character of the station scene over nearly a century and a half of railways. Our selection shows both the typical and the unusual, and we hope that this record may have some historical value as well, for only a handful of the stations illustrated have escaped major alteration or, in many cases, complete demolition.

Gordon Biddle
Jeoffry Spence

January 1977

Britain's widest single-span station roof is at St Pancras, completed in 1868 to the designs of W. H. Barlow and R. M. Ordish to house the Midland Railway's terminus and, with Gilbert Scott's hotel of 1874, to mark the company's entry into London. The giant latticed spans have no ties, a function performed by the platform foundations which are at first floor level on arches over bonded stores below.

INTRODUCTION

The *Concise Oxford Dictionary* describes a railway station as a 'stopping-place on railway with buildings for accommodation of passengers & goods. . . .' This may appear to be a somewhat old-fashioned description to today's user of the bus shelter type of accommodation, for it produces a picture of comparatively large, solid Victorian buildings, with various well-appointed rooms for first-class passengers, and more austere rooms for second- and third-class passengers, refreshment rooms, staff rooms and other offices. (One wayside station in Sussex, closed many years ago – and now a private house – with no population in the area on which to draw for its passenger traffic had, and still has, a subway between the platforms and *seven* lavatories).

In early days, only the more important stations had reasonable accommodation, and in many cases there was nothing at all; they were simply 'stopping-places'. With luck, a small hut might have been provided. In one instance, if historians are correct, a hollow oak tree did duty for booking purposes if not accommodation. This was at Moreton-on-Lugg on the Shrewsbury & Hereford Railway as late as the 1860s when the GW & LNW Joint Railways were rebuilding the station.

In some cases inns solved the problem of accommodation. If there was no inn by the station one very soon appeared, and although The Railway became only too common (there were only eight in London in 1864), Station, Locomotive and Junction also became stock names. Some old-established inns like Coach & Horses added & Railway just to make sure they were up to date. Others took the name of the railway company, as did the Eastern Counties at King's Lynn and the London, Chatham & Dover Railway – surely the longest inn name? – at Battersea.

In the important centres, and even the larger country towns, where there was civic pride in the local buildings, the station had to compete. Not only had it to be architecturally in keeping with the area, it had to look as solid and permanent as the company itself was supposed to be, for investors in railways often needed reassurance. Unfortunately – in some ways – stations were built to last and tended to become out of date according to a later and more modern image. It was all very well for the Victorians to have large, lofty rooms, with delightful but dust-harbouring mouldings, but they had the staff to heat and clean them, a matter which is a particularly sore point in this clinical age where cleanliness, although still next to godliness, is on the other side of it.

In the siting of the British station one comes across a weaker aspect of the railway system. So often was it placed in a position convenient to the railway company, but awkward for the customer. Road competition, and particularly the gradual expansion of country bus services during the first half of this century, would have drawn off only a certain amount of short distance traffic, but it set down or picked up the passenger and his luggage in the centre of the town. The only other competition could have come from a rival railway which, by running at a different level and perhaps by a better surveyed route, was able to place its station in a more central position.

One of the curiosities of some railways – and probably unique as a railway practice anywhere else – was the 'Road' station, which usually indicated a long walk or drive to the town. The Great Western in particular had a number of these stations, such as Bodmin Road, and were honest enough to indicate it, which is more than could be said for the South Eastern, a great many of whose stations were a very long way from the places they were supposed to serve. In the usual British fashion there was the other extreme with 'Road' stations which were really nothing of the sort, like Morton Road on the Great Northern which was virtually in the village of Morton-by-Bourne and had been named Morton until the 1880s.

One of the most daunting of the early 'Road' stations must have been Lampeter Road (later Llanwrda) on the Vale of Towy Railway, where the thought of a 16 mile trek over a couple of mountain ranges on a wild, wet Welsh night must have made the stoutest spirit quail. And who, knowing the commuter belt of suburban Purley, would think that in the 1840s the only name that could be thought up for a wayside platform was Godstone Road, that village being a good seven miles distant.

'Junction' was another word that came into general use for railways and their stations. There was a vague sense of importance about the denomination, but it could be misleading. Brampton Junction, on the Newcastle & Carlisle line became junctionless in 1923, and it was only in recent years that the name was put right. In 1928 the Southern Railway made a clean sweep of all 'junction' suffixes, other than those which were actually the junction for the place of the same name, as in Sidmouth Junction. Only two were left in the earlier category, Clapham Junction and Norwood Junction, which were too well established to be dispensed with, even if they were not really *at* those places.

Nomenclature is one of the odd but interesting sidelines of railway stations. The main object of naming a station, one would think, would be to indicate that the passenger had arrived at the place to which he had booked, but even the most intelligent passenger could encounter pitfalls. On the North Eastern Railway, for instance, that company was bequeathed by absorbed lines four stations by the name of Sherburn. From April 1874 this problem was partly solved by renaming the York, Newcastle & Berwick station Sherburn Colliery, and that of the Durham & Sunderland Sherburn House. Sherburn on the York and Leeds line remained until it became Sherburn-in-Elmet in July 1903. This left only one more to be disposed of, that on the York and Scarborough line. It was renamed Wykeham, a village about four miles north-east, but with the opening of the Pickering and Seamer line on 1 May 1882 a station was provided at Wykeham, which left officials to ponder on what to call the earlier Wykeham. All they could think of was Weaverthorpe, a village which lay about five miles south-east of the station. One of the social changes brought about by the railway was the way in which a new town grew up around the station, as in the case of Woking. The new town was as recently as 1922 shown on some maps by the name of Woking Station. In Ross-shire, Nigg Station has its own post office and telephone exchange, and is several miles from Nigg.

Station nameboards were an important feature and there was a wide variety of types. It is with some regret that present day standardisation can hardly be described as exciting. Names were usually on large wooden boards, held by upright posts often surmounted by finials, and placed at each end of the platform. If the passenger missed it he might be lucky to find additional signs etched into the glass of the lamps and illuminated, although feebly, at night. Some of the boards were massive: the ones at Tyseley – more a suburban than a junction station – advised the traveller from, say, Acocks Green, to change for, amongst other places, Exeter and Plymouth. It seems much more likely that any local passenger would have travelled to such distant places by first going into Birmingham to catch a fast train. An even more extreme example at Cheltenham is illustrated opposite.

The layout of the ordinary wayside station was simple. For a double line there was an up platform and a down platform. There was usually a siding and a small goods shed even at the most rural station, for in the heyday of railways there would be plenty of goods and coal traffic coming in, with local and agricultural traffic going out. Many junction stations had a bay for the branch trains, more often than not exposed to the weather, but an example of an overall roofed bay was at Tiverton Junction (see page 48), long since deprived of its branches. There seems to be some reluctance to change its name, though, in spite of the fact that unwitting passengers arrive there from time to time under the impression that they are at Tiverton. There were other curiosities, like the stations with staggered platforms, often on each side of a crossing and much favoured by the South Eastern. Some of the larger early stations had only one long platform, which up trains used at one end and down trains at the other, with crossover points in the middle. Brunel, in particular, used this type, but operating difficulties led to the construction of a second or more platforms, although Reading was not altered until 1899, and Cambridge still has only one platform to this day.

Some termini, too, at first were constructed with the offices ranged down one side like Paddington (where they still exist) and the early Euston, although the head-type of station, with a cross-platform – later a concourse – and the

The simple, basic profile of the overall station roof contrasts strongly with the ridge-and-furrow awning which evolved with particularly exuserant detail on the Midland Railway. Equally typical was the articulation of the blind arcading in the rear screen walls, shown in this photograph at Cheltenham Lansdown about 1905. In the background the signal-box crouches beneath the old overall roof of the original Birmingham & Gloucester Railway station, while the impressive list of destinations on the right could be reached, given time, by changing to the Midland & South Western Junction Railway.

British Railways

offices placed at right angles across the terminal end, was quickly realised to be a much more convenient arrangement. A number of country termini would be regarded as temporary, cheaply built and with limited accommodation, because it was the eventual intention to extend the line onwards. To do this from a station in use was not always possible without great inconvenience, and a diversion would be made, starting a short distance from the old terminus, with a new station – 'this commodious and imposing permanent structure' – in a more convenient position, with any luck, or a long way out of the town if not. The old station would then become

the goods station. An example of this was the Brighton company's station at East Grinstead, to which town a branch from Three Bridges was opened in 1855; the terminal station was very ordinary. In 1866 the line was extended to Tunbridge Wells, and a new through station of solid construction was opened a little nearer the town, and beside the main London to Lewes road. On the opening of the Croydon, Oxted & East Grinstead Railway in 1882, the station for this line was below and at right angles to the Tunbridge Wells line. As it was obviously more convenient to have a station on the high level above at the same location as the low level line to allow pas-

9

The forecourt of Derby station in 1906 presents an animated scene with cabs, open carriages and a waggonette vying with the new electric tramcar. The station is decorated for the Royal Show held at Derby in that year.
British Railways

senger interchange the second station on the Tunbridge Wells line was moved once again, even further away from the town than the first one had been. For some reason it was not until October 1883 that station No 2 was finally closed, so for more than 12 months both stations had been in use, some trains using one and some the other, which must have been infuriating for the stranger. There are numerous cases all over Britain of temporary termini; in some instances they were temporary for many years.

Some well known architects were employed by the railways, among them Sir William Tite, Edward M. Barry and Sir Gilbert Scott. Others were lesser known, even unknown outside their own field, but furnished work which was well

proportioned, imaginative, suited to its purpose and fitted into its environment with sympathetic use of local materials. Many were small town or local architects, like Frederick Barnes of Ipswich and Benjamin Green of Newcastle; others covered a wider field, for example Sancton Wood, who did work in England and Ireland, and Francis Thompson who worked on the North Midland, Chester & Holyhead, and Eastern Counties Railways. Again, others such as George Townsend Andrews and William Tress became identified with a particular company – the North Eastern and South Eastern respectively. Finally, there were the engineer-architects, men who with equal facility designed bridges, tunnels, stations and much else besides. Among them are great names like Isambard Kingdom Brunel and Robert Stephenson; on a slightly less prolific scale, the virtually unknown J. S. Crossley, who was responsible for much standardised station building on the Midland Railway, and William Peachey, who designed the magnificent roof at Middlesbrough.

Halts, now almost a thing of the past as suffix to the name, are part of railway station history. There has never been a really satisfactory explanation of them, or no explanation that would cover all the exceptions. Perhaps as good as any was H. F. Ellis's in *Punch* when he wrote that they were usually made of wood and 'because of their construction you can see beneath them and might even, if in holiday mood, crawl underneath from end to end – a quite impossible feat at Liverpool Street or Southampton. . . .' The Midland even had a Halt as a terminus, for the Harpenden–Hemel Hempstead branch trains actually finished their trips at Heath Park Halt. In 1903, 'push-and-pull' trains or 'steam rail motors' appeared for the first time. From 12 October the Great Western started a 'railway motor-car' service between Chalford and Stonehouse and additional stops were made at certain points other than the regular stations. At first there were no proper platforms at these new halts, and the vestibule at the end of the car was provided with steps by which passengers could alight or enter at the level crossings. Tickets were issued on the train itself. Within two years a number of other companies had adopted the idea – the Midland between Morecambe and Heysham Harbour from 11 July 1904, on the Glasgow & South Western between Mauchline and Catrine from 12 September 1904, on the North Eastern from Billingham Junction to Port Clarence (with a 'petrol-electric autocar') from 1 December 1904, and others. Timetables made a special note about them: 'These places are "Haltes"', a word imported from Belgium, and an affectation that lasted only a short time. By 1910 there were over 350 halts, including a few that used the suffix 'Platform'. Halt and Platform were similar, but Platforms were usually staffed (they first made their appearance on the Highland Railway in the mid-1870s). In the 1920s, with increasing competition from buses and cars, halts became an economy. There was very little expense and they performed a useful service to smaller villages. Now everything is altered: the present British Rail timetable lists only seven halts, two on the Romney, Hythe & Dymchurch Railway and five in Scotland. With so many wayside stations becoming unstaffed

halts there is little point in identifying them in any special way.

Dotted over the country were 'special' stations – royal, private, excursion, racecourse, works and factories, to name a few. Royalty was served exclusively at Gosport, at a supplementary station of simple design by William Tite, inside the Royal Dockyard. His South Western station at Windsor was a different matter, and superior to the one Brunel had designed for the Great Western. Tite's station had a curved single span trainshed with separate, richly designed accommodation for the Queen, topped by a bell-tower from which the staff could be warned of her approach. The royal station for Sandringham was at Wolferton, where the Great Eastern used pseudo half-timbering and a rustic styled 'lychgate' of a carriage porch on a separate royal building. Even the platform lamps were surmounted by gilded crowns. The Midland & Great Northern could hardly compete with their Hillington for Sandringham station.

Stations were provided by the railways in many cases for the nobility and gentry and these private stations naturally did not often appear in the public timetables. They were usually built at the demand of the landowner over whose ground the line passed, and the provision of a station was frequently one of the stipulations in return for an easy passage of the parliamentary Bill for construction of the line. Some private stations were, paradoxically, open to the public. Easton Lodge, near Dunmow, was opened for the Countess of Warwick, a standard Great Eastern wooden affair of which she could well have disapproved. The Countess was something of a martinet who also owned Gatton Park in Surrey, for which the original Merstham station was provided. This station, although built and opened by the London & Brighton Railway, was handed over to the South Eastern, with the $5\frac{3}{4}$ mile section from Stoat's Nest to Red Hill, when that company opened to Tunbridge in 1842, both companies using the same line as far as Redhill. The Countess was very angry with the South Eastern directors who, on taking over, closed the station with the intention of replacing it with the present station $\frac{1}{4}$ mile north, the opening of which was so delayed that she made legal representations. The company was forced to reopen the old station in October 1844, and the new one was not opened until the following year. Power meant a lot in the 19th century.

Dunrobin, on the Highland line to Wick, was the station for the nearby seat of the Sutherland family, and was the original terminus of the

The North Eastern Railway produced some of the most intricate ironwork. Tynemouth's riotous assemblage is shown with floral adornments for a special occasion.

then isolated Duke of Sutherland's Railway to West Helmsdale. It had the distinction, probably unique, of always appearing in the public timetables, but shown as 'Private', in brackets. The original station building, replaced by the present structure in 1902, was of Scots pine and stood on a long platform – long, that is, for a private station, for a great many guests would often be set down there in the old days of lavish entertainment. Dunrobin could almost be classified

as a royal station, and was more than once visited by kings, queens and emperors. Boreham was a private station built for Sir John Tyssen Tyrell, about three miles north of Chelmsford, on extension of the Eastern Counties Railway from Brentwood to Colchester in 1843. Sir John had alleged 'injury to his property' and the railway company gave him the right to stop any train there, a privilege not embodied in the Act, but entered into as a legal agreement. This lasted

during Sir John's lifetime, and he made full use of the facility until he died in 1877. The decencies and proprieties of the Victorian era were observed until the funeral two days later. The next day a gang of men appeared and demolished the station.

Special excursion stations were provided at resorts where traffic was heavy. Scarborough's was at Londesborough Road, several minutes walk from the Central station. At the other end

of the country, Weston-super-Mare had its own excursion station at Locking Road, and was shown in the public timetables. It was used, rather surprisingly, as a starting point and terminus of the Bristolian on summer Saturdays in 1952. The Blackpool stations had a number of excursion platforms, which were put to good use in the days before bus, coach and car took over. Racecourse stations were provided, for racegoers only, at Gatwick, Newbury and Aintree, among others. Tattenham Corner station was opened in 1901, with a public daily service until 1914 when, presumably because of the exigencies of war, it was closed except on race days, and not fully reopened until the line was electrified in 1928. Racecourse stations could be a headache for operating staff, for trains usually had to be stabled after arrival of racegoers, joyful in anticipation, and be ready to take everyone away, often in a hurry and sometimes dejected by the result of the day's sport.

There was a never ending source of entertainment at a country junction when waiting for the train; the arrival of the branch train at the bay platform, with its bustle of passengers, and off-loading of luggage and perishable traffic. In hindsight, even the noise of milk churns has a nostalgic clang about it. Among the smaller pieces of station equipment were luggage label cupboards, always a source of excursive pleasure for the inquisitive, containing pigeon-holes for labels for numerous destinations. The London, Brighton & South Coast in particular rather overdid this by having labels issued between each pair of stations on the system, which surely was not economic where paper was concerned. Almost up to its closing, Hartfield had labels for Keymer Junction, Caterham Junction, Hassock's Gate and other places, the names of which had long disappeared in one way or another. Familiar, too, were the clocks, especially the 'English Dial' often to be seen in the booking office or entrance hall, and so like the equally familiar kitchen clock. They kept good time, an important feature of the old railway systems. Today, so much is worked by electricity, that consequent blackouts, lockouts, strikes and other failures mean that a passenger can never feel entirely certain that the station clock is working, particularly when an announcement is made (probably electrically recorded) that his next train has been cancelled.

Then there were the notices warning against trespassing, instructing passengers to Cross the Line by the Bridge Only, or, in the case of the Great Western, not to make improper use of the fire buckets. Hanging above the platform at Tebay, among other stations, was a notice which read:

> THE RINGING OF THIS
> BELL INDICATES THE
> APPROACH OF A TRAIN
> WHICH DOES NOT STOP
> AT THIS STATION

As trains approached Tebay at high speed this was a reasonable, though, probably to the layman, useless, piece of information, useless, that is, until he was nearly swept off his feet by a passing train.

There were always the posters to look at, posters of Bridlington and Brighton, Morecambe and Margate, of green fields surrounding an ancient church (the church may still be there, but the fields have often been replaced by rows of chimneyless boxes of houses and petrol stations), of an elegant, dimpled lady, with enormous hat and bosom, luring you to unexpected destinations. One could inspect and memorise the type of 'dags' (decorative wooden pendants) on the awning valance to compare with other stations; and the number of permutations seemed limitless. One could even, if the train was very late and one suffered from this common psychological trait, walk all the way round and count them.

There was the temptation of the refreshment room. They were heavily panelled in dark wood, and contained a wide, solid counter, very likely marble-topped, with glass cases filled with piles of rather revolting-looking Madeira cake, Bath buns and dry sandwiches (the curling railway sandwich was, unfortunately, not a myth). The heavy décor has been replaced by something much more cheerful with which no one should grumble. Only the sandwiches have gone to the other extreme and are made with soggy, indigestible india rubber-type bread; no one seems to have thought of providing the colourful open sandwich on which can be placed some quite exotic foods. The London, Brighton & South Coast probably had more refreshment rooms, in proportion to the number of stations, than any other company, and one – sometimes more – was provided at all junction stations. The Great Eastern and the Midland provided, generally speaking, the best food, and the Scottish lines gave the largest meals, as befitted a nation of no-nonsense eaters and drinkers.

At the beginning of 1923 most companies were merged into the four groups – the GWR, LMS, LNER and Southern, with a small residue of miscellaneous joint and independent railways. About this time, though not for that reason, railway traffic began to decline. Motor-buses and coaches, which had been used by the North Eastern Railway for many years as an ancillary service, and by other companies to a lesser extent, were beginning to nose their way into the passenger receipts. Moreover motor cars were not the rare newfangled vehicles of 20 years before.

Railway managements, particularly some in high places, were inclined to rest on the laurels of the golden days. The motor, to them, was convenient for bringing passengers *to* a station. But with a fixed track, and stations not always conveniently placed, the passenger was becoming more and more content to travel the whole distance by road, at any rate for comparatively short journeys. When the railways began to fight back it was too late. The economically difficult years of the late 1920s and early 1930s took their toll in any case, and passenger services began to be withdrawn and stations closed. Many were on lines which should never have been built in the first place, and fierce and unremunerative competition between rival companies must often be blamed. The war, nationalisation and Dr Beeching accounted for the rest.

Architecture between the wars, for most new and rebuilt stations, was strictly functional, with much ferro-concrete. Although a number of designs were good many people did not like the new stations, for a good deal of 1930s artistry was decidedly vulgar. The new Euston of the late 1960s although more compact and convenient for passengers than the old, is far more impersonal than the rambling London & North Western station, with its odd nooks and crannies, dark corners and trolleys loaded with parcels which unexpectedly blocked the way of hurrying passengers. The main blot on the old station was the clutter of reservation offices which the LMS built right in the centre of the magnificent Great Hall, demolished alas with the rest of the old station.

What of the atmosphere at stations? So many memories can crowd back, from the bustle and unique smells (depending on the origin of the coal) of the great London termini to the windswept, rain-washed country station in the Scottish Highlands; from the stationmaster's trim garden in East Anglia, to the stations by the red sands and sparkling sea of the South Devon coast. Almost everywhere a station had a kind of soul, an atmosphere, which created – not least for the young – a sense of fun and adventure. Today there is so much slovenliness and indifference, and however much one might have complained in the past, sometimes with justice, of the dirt, or smell, or incompetence that could so often be found, in some way it is the untidiness of railway stations which lingers on in an affectionate memory. Perhaps we are just growing old.

London & Birmingham Railway lamp at the old Euston.

Above: The early passenger railways followed stage coach practice by using inns and hotels for booking tickets. At Abingdon Road (later Culham) in 1844 the Great Western appears at first to have used a toll-house as a booking office. The siding on the right probably indicates that the barn or stable also did duty as goods shed.

National Railway Museum

1 ORIGINS

Below: Likewise, the Leicester & Swannington Railway of 1832 used a room in the Ashby Road Hotel for its Bardon Hill station, shown here still in use by the railway in 1952, although in ruinous condition. *L&GRP*

Above: As the need for purpose-built premises became clear, small, simple buildings of local design and materials were erected as wayside stations. Heighington, on the Stockton & Darlington Railway; with its low cobbled platform, in reality is a two-storey structure built against an embankment with living quarters below.

Below: Another early line, the Grand Junction Railway (1837), built intermediate stations from the outset, like this 1964 survivor at Moore, comprising booking office and waiting room, with a separate station house behind.

Above: On other lines the crudest of wooden huts was considered sufficient. Some, like Sough on the Bolton, Blackburn, Clitheroe & West Yorkshire Railway, lasted surprisingly long. The story goes that this tarpaulin-covered shack was accidentally pulled down when caught by the coat buttonhole of a hurrying passenger. Judging from this picture, taken about 1860, it seems quite possible. *Darwen Public Library*

Below: Many of the early termini accommodated goods and passengers in a single establishment. Dundee (Ward) was one of Scotland's first passenger stations (1831). The passenger platform is on the right and the goods department on the left.

Above: The Liverpool & Manchester Railway's stations were a class apart, spaciously built in different styles. Edge Hill had matching two-storey buildings in local sandstone, with cornice and balconies from which the stationmaster could survey his domain. This engraving was made probably shortly after formation of the London & North Western Railway and the addition of the overall roof.
National Railway Museum

Above: The expression of reassurance for the timid traveller inherent in the humble, familiar features of the small wayside stations contrasted strongly with the big city stations. In them the new railways demonstrated their pride in achievement by erecting huge entrance buildings reflecting the social influences of the time. The eighteenth century classical revival provided an ideally monumental style to represent the new era of railways, typified by the giant columns of Euston, Newcastle and Monkwearmouth. The most perfect of them all is the magnificent Corinthian frontage of Huddersfield (1847), 416 ft long, by J. P. Pritchett Sr., of which the central portico is shown here after cleaning in 1972. It flanked a long single platform, in the manner of many early stations.

2 ARCHITECTS AND RAILWAYS

Below: Smaller but equally symbolic classical stations were built by the Midland Counties Railway at Nottingham and Leicester Campbell Street (1840), the latter seen here after its replacement by London Road station in 1896.

Above: Among the well known architects employed by railways the most prolific was Sir William Tite, who combined classical and Italianate forms in the London & Southampton Railway's termini. This is the 1839 Southampton Terminus photographed in the 1890s, and was the counterpart of Nine Elms in London, both head-type stations in which the frontage block stood directly behind the buffer stops.

Like his contemporaries, Tite was nothing if not versatile when it came to choosing styles. For his Eastern Counties Railway terminus at North Woolwich (1847) (*top right*), another head-type station, he used a restrained form of Italianate, while at Windsor & Eton Riverside (*right*) for the London & South Western he built an exceedingly fine neo-Tudor station in 1851, complete with separate Royal entrance and waiting room. *G. Biddle; R. E. G. Read*

Above: Tite's pupil, William Tress, designed stations for the South Eastern Railway, again mostly Italianate. But for Battle (1852), and its abbey, he evidently considered that only Gothic was suitable, complete with lancet windows and tracery — one of the finest stations we have in this style.   *R. E. G. Read*

Below: Italianate, too, was the choice of Sancton Wood for the terminus of the Eastern Counties Railway at Shoreditch (1844) with its flight of imposingly balustraded stairs. The head of the station here was formed by the company's offices, passengers entering beneath the covered drive at the side, shown here in the 1850s after formation of the Great Eastern.

National Railway Museum

Above: Francis Thompson designed some exquisite small stations. Wingfield, on the North Midland Railway, was charmingly symmetrical, neat and exactly proportioned, qualities still evident, despite 113 years' grime, in 1953.
R. E. G. Read

Below: At Chester General (1848) he built a long — over 1000ft — strongly Italianate frontage for another single sided station, punctuated by low towers, arcaded wings and a shallow tiled roof. It is generally regarded as his best large station.
R. E. G. Read

Left: Some architects were notable for adhering to a narrow range of styling which often characterised the line as well. J. W. Livock designed outstanding Tudor and Jacobean stations which hall-marked the Northampton–Peterborough and Rugby–Stafford lines of the London & North Western Railway. Simple flat awnings acted as a foil to his elaborate buildings, like this one at Northampton Bridge Street (1845), the scrolled brackets making a perfect union. *R. E. G. Read*

Above: Ipswich architect Frederick Barnes designed some noble stations for the Ipswich & Bury Railway, his finest at Bury St Edmunds (1846) combining a handsome Tudor centrepiece with an elevated, Renaissance-styled trainshed and a pair of domed towers – a seemingly incompatible blend which worked, seen here in the 1870s.

Below: The same individuality also marked stations on the Newcastle & Berwick Railway by Benjamin Green. The proportions of Beal (1847) verged on the manorial.

Above: Chatteris (1848), which later became part of the Great Northern & Great Eastern Joint line, was an example of how a simple country station building could be transformed by the addition of a Romanesque arcade instead of an awning, corner pilasters and a deep stone-mullioned window for the stationmaster's office. The frontage was a smaller edition. *R. E. G. Read*

Below: Of all our smaller stations, Newmarket's original terminus, on the Newmarket & Chesterford Railway (1848), was unique for the splendour of its proportions and finely detailed ornamentation. Nothing quite like it appeared elsewhere, yet it was merely the end of a branch line. *R. E. G. Read*

Above: David Mocatta designed the first unit stations on the London & Brighton Railway (1841), each based on a standard five-bay plan with a covered waiting area to the platform, but with variations in style. Merstham lasted only until 1845, but was photographed here still standing in 1939.

Below: I. K. Brunel was engineer, shipbuilder and architect all in one. Many of his stations for the Great Western Railway also revealed uniform features, like Aynho (1852). Characteristic are the neat matching buildings in local stone with all-round awnings decorated with lead lions' masks. *British Railways*

Best known of Brunel's designs were his wooden train-sheds. Here are two termini: Salisbury (*above*), opened in 1856, shows the series of pillars and cross-bracings supporting the roof over the side aisles (photographed in 1925), while the view of Merthyr Tydfil (*below*), opened in 1851, indicates a span wide enough to allow a central platform later, albeit propped up and near the end of its life. The gracefully glazed end-screen is also typical.
British Railways (both)

Jacobean doorway detail, Worksop.

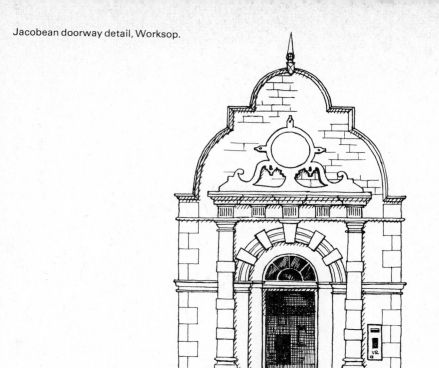

3 THE GRAND MANNER

Below: As the 19th century progressed, taste in building became both coarser and more elaborate. Old disciplines relaxed and styles were freely mixed. Matthew Digby Wyatt produced this incredibly flamboyant, spiky creation in French Gothic mixed with English Tudor at Bristol Temple Meads in 1878.

Left: Company styles began to emerge, too, the London, Brighton & South Coast Railway favouring a form of French-Italianate quite their own, seen in a particularly ebullient fashion at Portsmouth & Southsea (1876), a station jointly owned with the London & South Western. The balustrade is a fine example of Victorian detailed ironwork.

The more prosperous smaller companies were not to be outdone in the opulence stakes, the North London in 1873 essaying a series of Venetian–Gothic warehouse-type stations of which Canonbury (*bottom left*) was one of the best. On the fringe of the Lake District the Furness Railway held a competition for its new Ulverston station (*below*), the winning design, completed in the same year, incorporating a lofty Italianate clock tower. The elegant glass and iron awnings were typical Furness work.

R. E. G. Read; G. Biddle

Interiors were equally lavish, particularly head offices and boardrooms. The London & North Western, like no other railway, conducted itself in the best traditions of the Victorian grand manner, epitomised at Euston by the Doric Arch, the Great Hall and the Shareholders' Room, the splendours of the latter being shown here. It was the only company to have a special room for shareholders' meetings, erected in 1846–9 to the designs of P. C. Hardwick. The exquisite ceiling and marble columns disappeared with the rest of the old Euston in the early 1960s, one of the worst acts of official vandalism this country has seen.
National Railway Museum

Another fine interior which has disappeared was the Great Hall at London's Cannon Street (1866). Much more florid than Euston, it illustrates the move away from the classic dignity of the first half of the century to the rumbustious free-for-all of later Victorian commercial architecture of which its designer, Edward M. Barry, was a foremost practitioner. It also eloquently expressed the free-for-all attitudes of competing railway companies, of which the South Eastern's chairman, Sir Edward Watkin, was a leading exponent. *National Railway Museum*

Right: Not all were so well endowed. A latecomer on the railway map, the Hull & Barnsley was an attempt to break a railway monopoly. Its terminus at Hull Cannon Street can best be described as a series of wooden huts (1885). Intended as a temporary structure, it became a permanent reminder of the pitfalls of ill-judged competition until the LNER closed it in 1932.

Left: Some chairmen were remembered more graphically. Here is the bust of John Pearson, of the Lancashire & Yorkshire Railway, outside Liverpool Exchange station.

Below: Even the smallest of railways had their moments. The offices of the Oswestry & Newtown Railway were suitably housed in the French Renaissance frontage block of Welshpool station (1860). The company lasted only from 1855 to 1864, when it became part of the Cambrian Railways, but the station remains as a reminder of the short-lived glories of a 43 mile line.   *R. E. G. Read*

Right: Many railways built hotels at their main stations, either as separate buildings or, more often, part of the main frontage block like J. W. Livock's Queens & North Western Hotel at Birmingham New Street (1854), seen here before detracting alterations were made in 1911. The station entrance was through the arcade beneath the projecting centrepiece.   *British Railways*

Above: The best known railway hotel, and the most exotic, was the Midland Grand at St Pancras (1873). The interior was as equally magnificent as Gilbert Scott's exterior. This is a sitting-room in one of the suites, with Britannia looking down from the ceiling. St Pancras was the apogee of High Victorian.

Above: A roof covering platforms and rails was considered essential at all important stations and a good many lesser ones too. Except on the Great Western, which clung to Brunel's wooden sheds for many years, timber roofs quickly gave way to light iron and glass. Francis Thompson and Robert Stephenson's elegant, airy roofs at Derby and Leeds were among the first, while Euston started a whole dynasty of pitched roofs which came to characterise London & North Western practice. The new roofs shown being erected at Preston's new station in 1880 bear the same type of glazed gable screens and colonnaded columns as Euston nearly 50 years before.

4 IRON AND GLASS

Below: Ugly longitudinal pitched roofs with slatted ends were built at several Midland Railway stations, notably Lincoln St Marks, Nottingham, and Leeds Wellington, shown here, with very little glass, so that the interior was dark and gloomy. They were completely uncharacteristic of this company, which generally attained a high standard, and at Leeds were replaced by individual awnings in the early 1930s.
British Railways

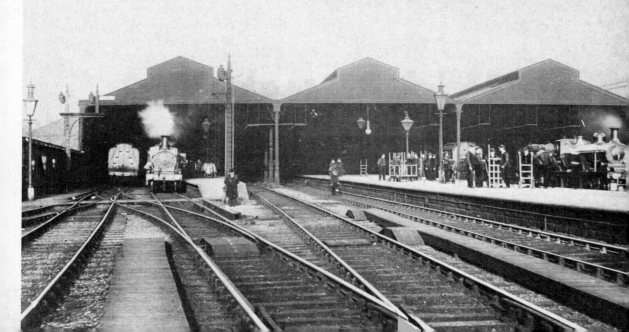

Above: Many stations grew piecemeal, none more so than the hotchpotch which was Waterloo before the London & South Western rebuilt it between 1907 and 1922. This is the concourse of the old south station about 1900 with its low roof, frilly valances and a motley collection of stalls, although the lamp globes are rather nice.

Below: The London, Brighton & South Coast Railway rebuilt Victoria between 1904 and 1908, replacing the old transverse iron and glass roof of 1860, shown here about 1900.

Above: None of these roofs was impressive in the manner of the lofty arched trainhalls which followed John Dobson's at Newcastle Central in 1849, based on Joseph Paxton's principles at Chatsworth House and used so successfully in the Crystal Palace. But they had fairly narrow spans — Newcastle's were 60ft — until E. A. Cowper designed his great crescent-trussed roof for Birmingham New Street in 1854, which, 210ft wide, was unsurpassed until the building of St Pancras. New Street is shown here in 1911 with its famous footbridge. *L&GRP*

Below: The second edition of Birmingham's other station, Snow Hill (1871), replacing a Brunel shed, had a much deeper crescent-trussed roof. This photograph shows it after removal of the gable screen in 1910, in readiness for demolition to make way for the third Snow Hill.
British Railways

In 1877 two important new stations were completed by the North Eastern Railway, both with enormously dramatic roofs. York (*top left*), by Thomas Prosser, had spans of five-centred arches on iron Corinthian columns supporting every third rib, the sharp curve of the station accentuating the arches of the roofs in a superlative series of perspectives. Middlesbrough (*left*), by William Peachey, was impressive for its great height, 60ft, in relation to its width, 74ft, and had a slightly pointed arch with no ties, springing directly from the platforms in a Gothic form which matched the buildings. It is seen here shortly before demolition following war damage.   *British Railways*

Above: At Perth the concourse was covered by an interesting pitched roof disguised by curved trusses and an attractive radial gable screen, photographed in the early 1900s.

Digby Wyatt's Gothic fantasy for the 1878 reconstruction of Bristol Temple Meads was matched by a Gothic arched trainshed, given emphasis, like York and Newcastle, by its site on a curve. The detailing of the gable glazing was par- ticularly fine although the interior lacked the clean lines of Middlesbrough and St Pancras because of the need for struts and ties.   *British Railways*

45

Left: For sheer dramatic effect, Liverpool Street is hard to beat. It was designed by the Great Eastern's engineer, Edward Wilson, and opened in 1874–5. Very high, light pitched roofs and curved trusses give an impression of an elliptical section, the interposition of steep-pointed aisles, transepts and vaulting lending it the unique atmosphere of some great iron and glass cathedral. The bow-windowed Edwardian tearoom, seen on the right, provides a charming contrast.   *The Architectural Review*

Above: Glass and iron were extensively used in platform awnings. The London & North Western adapted its Euston-type roof to a number of stations, including Penrith, shown here about 1926 with the typical arcade effect of the bracket spandrels and circles.

 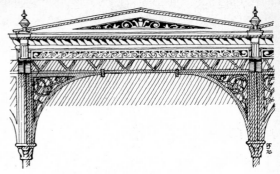

Above left: London, Tilbury & Southend Railway mono-grammed roof brackets at Westcliff-on-Sea.

Above right: Awning ironwork, Holyhead.

5 JUNCTIONS, BRANCHES AND WAYSIDE STATIONS

Below: Junction station layouts varied enormously. Separate platforms were provided at Tiverton Junction: on the left, there is a special short overall roof to house the Tiverton branch train, but the Hemyock branch platform on the right is open. The Great Western rebuilt the station in 1932.   *British Railways*

Above: This view of the old Newport, Abergavenny & Hereford Railway station at Pontypool Road in 1909 shows the island platform used by the Neath and Swansea trains. This station, too, was later rebuilt by the Great Western.   *British Railways*

Below: Some junction stations were built in the angle of the diverging routes, like Accrington on the Lancashire & Yorkshire Railway. The staff are lined up across the lines to Manchester on the left and Blackburn on the right.
Accrington Public Library

There were even stations with platforms on all three sides of a triangular junction. Ambergate was one of them, shown with a Midland train leaving for Manchester.

British Railways

Stations which originally were not junctions often had to make do with their existing platforms when a later line was built, like Evercreech Junction on the Somerset & Dorset Joint Railway (*above*). The generous width is a reminder that the line was intended to be Great Western broad gauge. Lampeter (*right*), on the erstwhile Manchester & Milford Railway, is shown a few years after the Great Western acquired it, with an Aberayron branch rail motor train strengthened with a pair of four-wheel coaches, perhaps on a market day. *J. G. Spence; British Railways*

Left: Branch lines had a charm of their own, added to by the ancient engine and coaches at Dursley about 1865, where a single platform formed the terminus.   *L&GRP*

Below: Accommodation was more generous at Abingdon's old station, including a wooden trainshed beneath which the branch train could be kept overnight.
British Railways

Above: Crook of Devon, on the North British Railway's Alloa–Kinross line, had no more than basic essentials: booking office, wooden waiting room, lamp room made from a redundant wagon body, and iron urinal. The goods department shared the same platform.

Below: Drayton for Costessey was a typical Midland & Great Northern Joint line station, with garden, slotted post signals and one of the M&GN's curious wooden cross-braced footbridges. The striped-painted valance is characteristic of a number of railways in the last century.
British Railways

Above: The Great Eastern's wooden buildings at Stonea were quite untypical, and more reminiscent of colonial styling than British practice. *British Railways*

Below: Cottage orné was a style beloved of the early Victorians, simulating the picturesque. The Shrewsbury & Chester Railway considered it suitable for Shropshire and adopted it in various forms. The barge-boards and finials at Baschurch were particularly elaborate, seen here shortly before removal of the turret by the Great Western in 1921. *British Railways*

Above: Cockermouth station had a group of substantial stone buildings with full facilities, including refreshment room, to serve the small Lake District town.

R. Sankey collection

Below: Furness Railway rainwater head, Bootle.

Below: Station offices were sited along one platform, often with only a small waiting shelter or awning on the other. Occasionally trouble was taken to ensure they matched, like this specimen at Frimley.

Right: Some verged on the bizarre, like this Byzantine building which contained the entrance to the District Railway's Blackfriars station in the 1870s.

Below: Architectural good manners deteriorated from the 1860s onward. The railways were no exception, in new work or the defacement of the old. This pleasant little Midland Railway station at Southwell was almost completely hidden by enamel advertisements in 1895. The place evidently was considered an expanding market for soap.

Top left: Standardisation also grew, so that the style of building bespoke a railway company as eloquently as its engines and rolling-stock. Here is Lofthouse & Outwood about 1906, another V-shaped junction station, with a typical Great Northern wooden building.
J. B. Sykes collection

Above: The London & North Western's wooden stations were strikingly neat, unmistakeable with their deep, flat awnings and, often, equal-sized buildings that 'balanced' on each platform, like Clifton Mill. *R. E. G. Read*

Left: Later, wooden buildings began to proliferate, with and without awnings, often assembled in a haphazard manner like the Barry Railway's collection at Barry Docks station in 1925. *British Railways*

Right: The Great Eastern's later stations were equally distinctive, with patterned tile-hung gables, curved-topped wing walls and serrated valance. Southminster, in 1889, was a representative example. *R. E. G. Read*

Above: Edward Walters designed a series of well appointed, handsome stations for the Midland Railway's line to Manchester from Matlock in 1863, like Bakewell, photographed about 1902 with its ample ridge-and-furrow glass awnings and characteristic two-way nameboard on the right. The design was repeated on the company's London extension south of Radlett.

Standardisation did not necessarily limit a company to one style although some, like the London & North Western, very largely did so. Sutton (*top left*), an outer London suburban station, was extended by the London, Brighton & South Coast Railway in 1882 with some of its flat awnings on plain brackets. Yet out in the country the same company built some extraordinarily opulent stations like Horsted Keynes (*bottom left*), shown newly completed in the same year, with pseudo half-timbering, floral parget-ting, elaborate porch with stained glass and a delicately fretted awning valance.

Below: The Cheshire Lines Committee, as behoved a joint line, imported into its stations something from two of its three owners. The general style and integral covered area at Heaton Mersey, photographed in 1904, are un-mistakeably Manchester, Sheffield & Lincolnshire Rail-way, while the elaborate gable bargeboards are distinctly Midland. Only Great Northern influence is missing, which perhaps was as well.

Above: For its London extension of 1899 the Great Central built the most completely uniform series of stations seen in this country. There were 22, with island platforms and, apart from three larger ones, all identical. Here is Charwelton, shortly after opening.

Leicester Museum, Newton collection

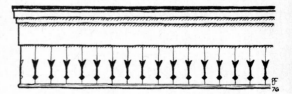

Above: London & North Western valance at Disley.

Below: Valance at Dorking North, London, Brighton & South Coast Railway.

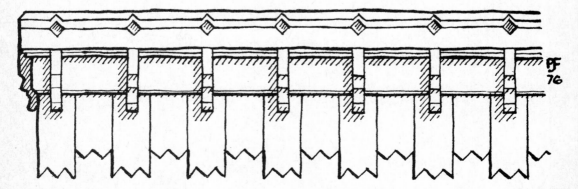

7 THE BIG FOUR AND BRITISH RAIL

The end of the 1914—18 war also saw the end of Victorian attitudes, architecture and railway companies. The last were amalgamated into four main groups. Architecture developed in three popular streams, one being a domestic style owing much to the revival of the 1880s, reflected in stations like Croxley (*above*) of 1925, on the Metropolitan & LNER Joint line to Watford, now part of London Transport. The steep roof and deep eaves also typified Beningbrough (*right*), rebuilt by the LNER when it widened its main line north of York in 1930—3, and notable for the matching signalbox which made a particularly pleasing and unusual ensemble.

G. Biddle; R. E. G. Read

Left: Neo-Georgian, beloved of banks, labour exchanges and the Post Office, was popular for larger stations. The Southern used it when it rebuilt Exeter Central and, shown here, Exmouth (1933), although the detailing is coarse compared with the real thing.

Below: The third style was a kind of debased classicism, heavy and chunky as though it were using children's building bricks, like the Great Western's new entrance block at Cardiff built in the early 1930s.   *British Railways*

As the 1930s progressed a completely new style of architecture emerged, forerunner of the functional forms of our own day. The Southern Railway built a large number of 'ultra modern' stations as they were then considered, under its architect J. R. Scott, as part of its 'Southern Electric' image. One of the foremost was Surbiton of 1937 (*above*). Guided by Frank Pick and Charles Holden the London Passenger Transport Board was equally forward looking in creating a new, unified approach to design in its New Works programmes in which many new stations were erected. Concrete, brick and glass predominated in the striking lines of East Finchley (*below*) built in 1939.

R. E. G. Read (both)

Although they did less new work, the other railways produced some advanced designs. Electrification was the spur to rebuilding some Wirral Railway stations by the LMS in 1938, leading to bold lines and curves at Hoylake (*above*) in reinforced concrete. The LNER promoted itself with a fish-shaped totem at stations built during this time, seen here at the new West Monkseaton station (*below*) on North Tyneside, where electrification went back to 1905. The flat-roofed building on the road bridge, more use of concrete and the globular lamps are typically 1930s.

L&GRP; R. E. G. Read

Above: Forty years later some of the pre-war ideas seem quaint, almost crude. The cubist-like murals around the concourse at Hastings were obviously thought the last word in modern design by the Southern, showing local beach scenes and prominent electric train. *R. E. G. Read*

The recent advent of new materials like plastics and the imaginative re-use of old materials have brought new dimensions into architecture. While there has been valid criticism of British Railways' 'basic railway' policy in reducing station structures to bus shelter dimensions, much of its major work has been highly commendable. The reconstruction of Manchester Oxford Road (*lower left*) in timber and concrete is an adventurous exercise in curved shapes, while Potters Bar (*below*) comprises equally refreshing straight lines with extensive use of glass.   *R. E. G. Read (both)*

Above: The functional frontage of Portishead was given texture by the thoughtful use of stone facings, with concrete platform awnings seen behind. The past tense is deliberate, for having rebuilt the station in 1954 British Rail closed it a few years later.   *R. E. G. Read*

Below: Tinted glass has been effectively deployed in one of British Rail's most recent reconstructions, Larbert, completed in 1976, while managing to maintain harmony with the old Caledonian Railway footbridge.   *British Railways*

8 FURNITURE AND APPOINTMENTS

Below: A wide variety of accessories was an essential part of the Victorian station scene, although much of the old is fast disappearing and smaller items have become collectors' pieces. This corner of Kemble station was like many a country junction: a pair of benches bearing GWR initials, the left hand one in its 1930s house style, with only the 'W' later painted in by BR; the heavy penny-in-the-slot weighing machine with brass handles; and the wooden telephone kiosk.   *R. E. G. Read*

Above: The old London & North Western wooden station at Banbury Merton Street, with its curved roof, retained its Victorian equipment to the end. The delightfully lettered nameboard, park bench seats, trolley, and gas lamps seem incongruous alongside the diesel railcar which still required sets of portable steps from the low platform. *R. E. G. Read*

Left: The North Eastern displayed maps of its system in glazed tiles at the more important stations. Some still remain, now carefully preserved. This one was photographed at Tynemouth.

Above: Station nameboards very properly were a prominent platform feature. Some of the early railways made them permanent fixtures, like the station names engraved on slate on the walls at Chester & Holyhead Railway stations. Others were less so – a painted board, albeit elaborately executed, was used by the South Eastern at Hope Mill, later renamed Goudhurst.

Below: Most companies eventually adopted screwed cast iron letters, the Cheshire Lines favouring an attractive serif style as shown at Cuddington, in six different sizes.
L&GRP

Top: After grouping the LMS, like London Transport, devised a distinctive standard sign. Farthinghoe is an example of a large one in light alloy, which was mounted on a sheet-steel backing in a wooden frame and painted yellow and black. Matching enamel plates were hung beneath the platform lamps, of which Smithy Bridge is an example. Culgaith is a modern lamp-sign in BR plastic.

Above: Train information was important at busy stations. This view of St James's Park on the District Railway depicts an early electrically illuminated destination indicator, the numbers showing the next train sequence. Some are still in use, although the attractive lamp globes have long since gone.

STALYBRIDGE JOINT STATION NOTICE

ALL PERSONS FOUND TRESPASSING OR LOITERING ON THESE PREMISES ARE LIABLE TO BE TAKEN INTO CUSTODY TO BE DEALT WITH ACCORDING TO LAW

——— BY ORDER

THE USE OF THIS WATER CLOSET CAN BE HAD ON PAYMENT OF ONE PENNY AT THE BOOKING OFFICE

DISTRICT RAILWAY.

NOTICE.

In the absence of the Ladies' Waiting Room Attendant the Station Inspector is authorised to look in occasionally to see that no improper use is made of this room.

(BY ORDER.)

Above: When it came to preventing mischief, Victorian propriety was strained. Although train spotters were yet to come, loiterers in general were discouraged in no uncertain terms. Managements were punctilious, too, about the status of a station, as the 'joint' notice at Stalybridge shows.

Left: One wonders what instructions were given to the booking clerk at the many North Eastern country stations where this notice was found. Did he unlock the door in person or merely hand over the key? Was a ticket issued as a receipt?

Bottom left: Even more intriguing is the potential which the District Railway obviously thought an unattended Ladies' Room offered. No doubt the card was hung in a discreet position.

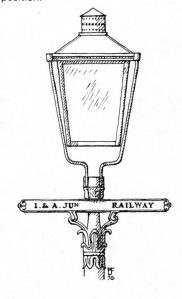

Right: Inverness & Aberdeen Junction Railway station lamp.

81

9 THE GOODS DEPARTMENT

Above: While passenger trains created the glamour, on most railways the goods department brought in the greater revenue, based on the sidings and goods shed without which no station, however small, was complete. Here is Newmarket, a typical country town goods station, with its central platform between rail and road and a pair of hand cranes for exchanging goods, all in a simple barn-like structure clearly derived from agricultural practice.
R. E. G. Read

Pages 84–5: In fundamentals the scene continued unchanged well into this century, the principal difference at Cardiff's Newtown goods station in the 1920s being a steel-framed building instead of timber, and electric overhead travelling cranes in place of hand-operated pillar cranes. Otherwise goods are still being manhandled across a central dock into horse-drawn drays, just as they were in 1841. Mechanical handling and freightliners were still some way off.

Above: The city goods depot presented a similar picture on a larger scale, like that at Bristol shown here in 1841.

Below: Externally, goods sheds were plain and unpretentious, like this Great Western brick and timber example at Wootton Bassett shown before the gauge change of 1892. The shunting horse, the old Brunel station building, the slotted semaphore signal and the disc and crossbar signal beyond the bridge, add value to a picture which changed with the rebuilding in 1902 and has now vanished completely. *British Railways*

Above: Not all goods depots were utilitarian. As befitted the Midland Railway, some delightful sheds were built which were at once functional — what more so than the weather protection afforded by the overhanging eaves at Helpston? — yet full of charm. The proportions have been applied with care while the little balconies concealing the hoist gears add a touch of delicacy.

R. E. G. Read

Below: Others were styled to match an adjacent passenger station and form a group, although few as elaborately as Hampton Court with its Gothic touches and buttressing, possibly by Sir William Tite who designed a number of the earlier London & South Western stations.

Above: Vast multi-storey warehouses were built to contain the raw materials and products of industry. Many can still be seen at the lineside, although generally now used for other purposes. Massive construction, often on fireproof principles, made them urban landmarks. Some were designed for special traffics, like the great fruit and vegetable, wool and cotton, or bonded goods stores in our large cities, reminders that nearly everything travelled by rail. This picture shows the loading chutes at Marsh Lane grain warehouse, Leeds, now demolished.

Below: Special wagons also were needed. Here a consignment of bicycles is being shunted outside Warwick Road goods station, Coventry, about 1912 when domination by the motor industry was still more than a decade away. The elaborate hoist housing, with its short frilly valance, was often found.

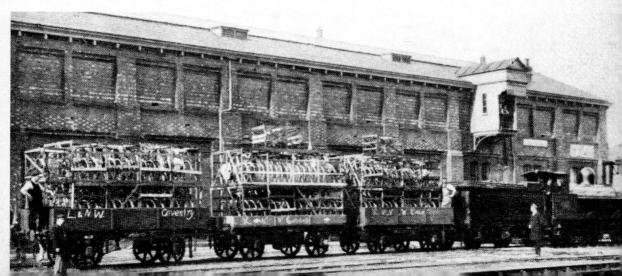

Right: The circus comes to town in a train of special vehicles: Barnum & Bailey unload their elephants outside the colonnade-like arches of Forth goods station, Newcastle-upon-Tyne, in the 1920s.

Below: On a humbler scale Ribble Valley farmers await the Manchester milk train outside Clitheroe station on the Lancashire & Yorkshire Railway. This daily event was a scene of fierce competition to be first to unload and thus first away.

Above: Goods yard capstan notice, Huddersfield.

10 MAKING A JOURNEY

Above: To our Victorian forebears a railway journey was at first an adventure and nearly always an event. This engraving of Slough in 1846, the station on the left and the hotel on the right, shows the bustle in the forecourt with passengers arriving by carriage, on horseback and on foot. The mounted troopers in the background probably indicate the expected arrival of the Queen, for this was then the station for Windsor. *National Railway Museum*

Below: In some instances railway companies provided their own conveyances, such as the Lancashire & Yorkshire's parcels and luggage van outside Sowerby Bridge station, with a privately-operated hansom for passengers. *David Joy collection*

Right: The cab trade quickly developed with the growth of railways. Every station of any size had its rank, like this lengthy one stretching up Terminus Road at Brighton in 1903.

Above: The tramcar brought changes: horse, steam, then electric. On the bridge outside Wolverton station this steam tram awaits passengers for Stony Stratford.
L&GRP

Booking offices varied from the tiny pigeonhole in a draughty passageway at a small station to the ecclesiastical interior of Kenilworth's booking hall (*below left*) and the shiny new terra-cotta with six windows at Nottingham Midland (*top right*) in 1906, completed two years before.
G. Biddle; British Railways

Right: Apart from fashions and loudspeakers, the concourse at Blackpool Central had changed little by 1934, the other elements — chocolate machines, enamelled advertisements and mobile buffet — being pre-first war. Although notice boards have been relettered 'LMS', the departure indicator still displays 'L&Y and L&NW Joint Railways' eleven years after their demise. This station site is now a car park.
British Railways

Above: Although by the time this photograph was taken in 1935 the old wooden Great Western trainshed at Banbury was a byword for dilapidation, it withstood the pounding of Birmingham expresses for 23 years more. The refreshment room still retains its 'First Class' distinction amidst the *art nouveau* glass, and, despite the clutter of signs and advertisements, Brunel's handsome roof struts still indicate past glories.　　　　　　　　　　*British Railways*

Right: Once the passenger was in possession of a ticket and safely on the platform, time awaiting the train could be spent at the bookstall. Here too there have been changes; many stations no longer have bookstalls, and W. H. Smith and John Menzies, who have the concessions on much of BR and London Transport, are modernising them at the remainder. W. H. Smith's establishment at Skipton in 1907 however is little different from that of today. Aproned tea-boys have disappeared but station staff nowadays again wear pill-box caps.　　　　　　　　　　*David Joy collection*

Below: Great Northern Railway monogram on fireplace, Peakirk.